If you were me and lived in...
SCOTLAND

A Child's Introduction to Culture Around the World

Carole P. Roman

For Brittney- my very first publicist.
Many thanks to Kelsea Wierenga.
Your illustrations are an inspiration!

Copyright © 2014 Carole P. Roman

All rights reserved.

ISBN: 1500531332

ISBN 13: 9781500531331

Library of Congress Control Number: 2014912690

CreateSpace Independent Publishing Platform

North Charleston, South Carolina

SCOTLAND

EDINBURGH

If you were me and lived in Scotland (Skot-land), your home would occupy the northern third of the island of Great Britain (Brit-an). It is part of the United Kingdom, which means it is a included in a group of countries from that area. They are England (Eng-land), Wales (Wails), Northern Ireland (Ay-er-land), and Scotland. Scotland has more than 790 islands in the North Sea.

2

You might live in the capital, Edinburgh (Ed-in-bruh). It is the second most populous city in Scotland. That means a lot of people live there. Edinburgh is famous for its university (uhn-i-ver-cit-ee), which teaches medicine, law, science, and engineering. People have lived in this spot for over ten thousand years. It is also known as the Athens (Ath-enz) of the North because many of the building are inspired by ancient Greece and Rome.

If you are a boy, your parents may decide on Ian (Ee-yan), Connor (Con-nor), or Malcomb (Mal-cum) as a name. They might choose Aillen (Aye-leen), Kelsey (Kel-see), or Margaret (Mar-gar-et) if you are a lass. Can you guess what being a lass means?

6

You would call your mommy, Mathair (May-their) and if you had to tell your daddy something, you could call him Dadadh (Dad-dah).

8

British pounds are the type of money used to buy things in the store, but you could also use Scottish notes when purchasing a stuffed unicorn (uhn-i-corn). Unicorns don't really exist. The mythological creature is the official animal of Scotland and was printed on coins many years ago. They picked the legendary beast because it represented grace, purity, healing, and happiness. Do you know what the official animal of your country is?

10

You might like to take a trip to Loch Ness (Loc Nes). It is a large freshwater lake in the Scottish Highlands and best known for the creature people say lives in the deep water.

She is called Nessie (Nes-see), and people wonder if she really exists. Many have claimed to have seen her and say she is as big as a dinosaur. There are no real pictures of her, so it's hard to prove she is really there. Either way, it's still a big mystery. What do you think?

Loch Ness is Scotland's second largest lake and very deep. It contains more freshwater than all the lakes in England and Wales combined. It is a beautiful vacation spot.

14

Every morning you would wake up to a steaming bowl of porridge made from oatmeal. You would eat that with tattie scones (tat-tee scoo-nes), which are tasty potato muffins. For lunch and dinner, you might like to eat cullen shink (cul-len shin-k), which is a hearty soup of the fish haddok (had-dok), potatoes, and onions. Another dish that is popular on cold nights is a stew called stovies (sto-vees). It's made with meat, potatoes, and onions. Maybe your parents would make haggis (hag-gis) on special occasions. It is a cooked, stuffed sheep's stomach filled with meat and spices. It is usually eaten on holidays. Oats are used in everything from stuffings to desserts. You would love to finish your meal with a Scottish tablet which is a fudge-like candy. Perhaps you'd like a clootie (cloo-tee) dumpling instead. It is a sweet pudding filled with raisins, sugar, milk, and syrup. Yum!

16

Your favorite sport would have to be golf. Golf (gol-f) is played on a large open field where you might try to get a small hard ball into a tiny hole with as few swings as possible. It takes a lot of practice. The first game of golf was played in Scotland sometime in the year 1457. Saint Andrews (An-droos) is a famous golf course.

When cousins come, you would ask your parents to go to the Highland Games. It is a multi-sport festival, celebrating all kinds of games that are popular in Scotland. You might dress as your ancestors did in kilts (kill-tiss), tartans (tar-tens), and plaids (pl-ades).

Kilts are wrap-around skirts that are the traditional dress of men. Tartans and plaids are woven cloths made exclusively in the colors and design for your family. If you are strong enough, you might try out in an event like the caber (cab-er) toss. You would balance a giant log in your hands, run a distance, and throw it. There is a lot of music with bagpipes (bag-pipes) and dancing.

You would tell all your friends about it in sgoil (s-g-oil).

22

So you see, if you were me, how life in Scotland could really be.

Pronunciation Guide

Aillen (Aye-leen)-popular girl's name.

Athens (Ath-enz) of the North-nickname for Scotland because it is so cultured and home of a great university.

bagpipes (bag-pipes)-musical instrument made with sheep's stomach and small flutes attached to it.

caber (cab-er)-sport from the Highland Games where a player carries a large pole and attempts to toss it far away.

clootie (cloo-tee)-pudding made with milk, raisins, fruit, sugar, and syrup.

Connor (Con-nor)-popular boy's name.

cullen shink (cul-len shin-k)-fish stew.

Dadadh (Dad-dah)-Dad.

Edinburgh (Ed-in-bruh)-capital of Scotland.

England (Eng-land)-one of the countries that are part of the United Kingdom.

golf (gol-f)-game played on large grassy course, where on tries to hid a small hard ball into a tiny hole with as few strokes as possible.

Great Britain (Brit-an)-the island that is made up of England, Scotland, and Wales.

haddock (had-dok)-white, flakey fish used in stew.

haggis (hag-his)-stuffed sheep's stomach filled with meat, oats, and onions.

Ian (Ee-yan)-popular boy's name.

Kelsey (Kel-see)-popular girl's name.

kilts (kill-tiss)-traditional wrap skirt worn by Scottish men.

Loch Ness (Loc Nes)-Scotland's second largest lake.

Malcomb (Mal-cum)-popular boy's name.

Margaret (Mar-gar-et)-popular girl's name.

Mathair (May-their)-Mommy.

Nessie (Nes-see)-legendary dinosaur-like beast that lives in the Loch Ness.

Northern Ireland (Ay-er-land)-a country part of the United Kingdom.

plaids (pl-ades)-a design on material that identifies the family.

Saint Andrews (S-aint An-droos)-a famous golf course in Scotland.

Scotland (Skot-land)-one of the countries that are part of the United Kingdom.

Scottish tablet (Skot-tish tab-let)-fudge-like candy.

sgoil (s-g-oil)-school.

stovies (sto-vees)-meat stew made with potatoes and onions.

tartens (tar-tens)-specially made designed woven cloth made specifically for a family.

tattie scones (tat-tee scoo-nes)- potato muffins.

unicorn (uhn-i-corn)-mythical creature that looks like a horse with a single horn on its head.

university (uhn-i-ver-cit-ee)- school that you attend after high school.

Wales (Wailes)- one of the countries that are part of the United Kingdom.

Made in the USA
Middletown, DE
27 January 2015